NATIONAL
GEOGRAPHIC

Servant to
ABIGAIL ADAMS

*The Early American Adventures
of Hannah Cooper*

Kate Connell

PICTURE CREDITS
Cover © Museum of the City of New York/CORBIS; cover (inset) and
page 6 (right inset) Smithsonian American Art Museum, Washington
DC/Art Resource, NY; pages 1, 4, 4–5, 12–17, 26–27, 30–33, 37 The
Granger Collection, NY; pages 2–3, 6–11, 18, 21, 34–35, 38–39
North Wind Picture Archives; pages 5 (inset), 28–29 Courtesy White
House Historical Association; page 6 (left inset) Roy Miles Gallery,
London, UK/Bridgeman Art Library; page 20 Culver Pictures; pages
22–25 Library of Congress; page 26 (top) Art by Louis
Glanzman/National Geographic Society.

Cover: New York City
Title page: President's House, 1807
Contents page: Washington, D.C. in 1800

ISBN: 0-7922-5828-2
CIP data available on request

Produced through the worldwide resources of the National
Geographic Society, John M. Fahey, Jr., President and Chief
Executive Officer; Gilbert M. Grosvenor, Chairman of the Board;
Nina D. Hoffman, Executive Vice President and President, Books and
Education Publishing; Ericka Markman, President, Children's Books
and Education Publishing Group; Steve Mico, Vice President
Education Publishing Group, Editorial Director; Marianne Hiland,
Editorial Manager; Anita Schwartz, Project Editor; Tara Peterson,
Editorial Assistant; Jim Hiscott, Design Manager; Linda McKnight,
Art Director; Diana Bourdrez, Anne Whittle, Photo Research;
Matt Wascavage, Manager of Publishing Services; Sean Philpotts,
Production Coordinator; Jane Ponton, Production Artist.

Production: Clifton M. Brown III, Manufacturing and Quality Control

PROGRAM DEVELOPMENT
Gare Thompson Associates, Inc.

BOOK DESIGN
Herman Adler Design

Published by the National Geographic Society
1145 17th Street, N.W.
Washington, D.C. 20036-4688

Printed in Spain

Table of Contents

INTRODUCTION   Two Hundred Years Ago in America   **4**

CHAPTER 1   The President's Household **7**

CHAPTER 2   A Shadow Over the Presidency **13**

CHAPTER 3   Summer in Quincy **21**

CHAPTER 4   The New American Capital **27**

CHAPTER 5   A New Beginning **35**

EPILOGUE **39**

GLOSSARY **40**

Two Hundred Years Ago in America

The United States in 1800 was a new nation. It was a **democracy**, a new experiment in government. In 1800, many people weren't sure how the experiment would turn out.

The first President had been George Washington. Elected in 1789, he served for eight years. Then he retired to Mount Vernon, his home in Virginia. He was a very popular president.

John Adams, elected in 1796, was the nation's second President. He and his wife, Abigail, lived in the nation's temporary capital—Philadelphia, Pennsylvania.

The Adamses had servants. They were often young women from families in their hometown, Quincy, Massachusetts. Not much is known of them. We can imagine that they were very much like 13-year-old Hannah Cooper. Her parents, Amos and Susan, lived in Quincy on a few poor acres of land. Her older brother, Daniel, was a printer's **apprentice** in New York City.

In those days, poorer families like the Coopers often sent their children out to work. Separated and far from home, Hannah and Daniel would have written letters. Their letters are like a window on an early America.

Abigail Adams

John Adams

BUILDING THE FIRST WHITE HOUSE

"I PRAY HEAVEN TO BESTOW THE BEST BLESSINGS ON THIS [WHITE] HOUSE, AND ON ALL THAT SHALL HEREAFTER INHABIT IT. MAY NONE BUT HONEST AND WISE MEN EVER RULE UNDER THIS ROOF!"

—JOHN ADAMS, NOVEMBER 2, 1800

WASHINGTON D.C. 1798

MEET THE COOPER CHILDREN

Hannah Cooper, 13

Daniel Cooper, 16

CHAPTER 1

The President's Household

In early October, 1799, Abigail Adams set out from Quincy to join her husband, John, in the capital, Philadelphia. She rode in a coach with her grown daughter, her little granddaughter, and her niece. Behind came a second coach carrying servants and bags and trunks.

It was not the first time Abigail had made this journey since her husband was elected President. In those days, most government officials didn't live in the capital all year. The summer climate was considered unhealthy. In May or June, government officials finished their business and went home. President and Mrs. Adams did the same. They spent summers in Quincy. They returned to the capital in late fall.

Thus it was that Hannah Cooper, Mrs. Adams' newest servant, found herself traveling far from home for the first time. Squeezed into the carriage with the other servants, she bumped along the road to New York. After a journey of about a month, they arrived in the pouring rain at the Executive Mansion in Philadelphia.

Philadelphia
December 3, 1799

Dear Daniel,

I hope this letter finds you well. I am in good health, except for a cough. It started when we arrived at this place. We came through a fearful downpour. I was soaked. Mrs. Adams gives me a tonic of sulfur, cream of tartar, and honey. It tastes horrible, but she makes me take it anyway.

My work here is much the same as at home, but this house is the grandest I've ever seen. It is a large mansion, all brick and very handsome. I am up soon after dawn and busy until night. I help in the kitchen, lay the table, bring tea trays, air the bedding, sweep, and attend to Mrs. Adams' wants.

I try to listen and remember all that Mrs. Adams tells me. She is demanding, though kind. Today I was very embarrassed. She sent me to her trunk for her silver-trimmed gown and it wasn't there. I had packed the wrong dresses! Oh she was sorely disappointed. It is important that she look the part of the President's wife. After a scolding, she said never mind. She is writing to her sister, Mrs. Cranch, to send them.

I know that you want to hear about politics. I am sorry I have nothing to tell you. Mr. Adams delivered his yearly address to Congress today at noon. But what he said to Congress, I know not.

I will close now. Wishing you good health, I remain,

Your affectionate sister,
Hannah

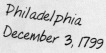

Philadelphia
December 3, 1799

Dear Mother and Father,

I write to tell you that we arrived safe about ten days ago. I hope you are both in good health and that the pain in your back has eased, Father. I think the herb pillow I made you will help.

This city is larger and noisier and busier than you could imagine. Our house is on the High Street, also called Market Street. There are many markets and shops. The streets are all of cobblestone, the sidewalks of brick. Gentlemen and ladies come and go all day long to see the President. Others come for Mrs. Adams' teas and dinners.

Mrs. Adams keeps a sharp eye on the household. She says she will send my wages every month. Mother, Mrs. Cranch will soon be sending some clothing to Mrs. Adams. If you brought her my doll, Beanie, do you think she would send her, too? If I had Beanie at night, I think I would not miss you and Father so much.

Your loving daughter,
Hannah

Old State House, Philadelphia   9

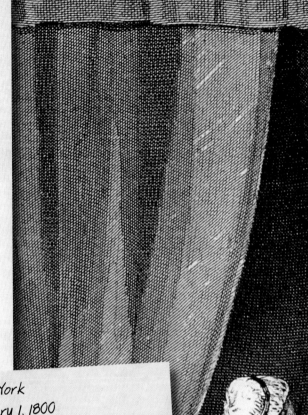

from Hannah Cooper's diary
December 18, 1799

Mother gave me this small book to record my thoughts. I've been saving it for something important. Now something important has happened: Mr. George Washington is dead. He died late on Saturday night at Mount Vernon.

Both President and Mrs. Adams were truly saddened by the news. All the ladies will wear white with black trimmings to show respect. Mrs. Adams says she can spare a piece of black ribbon for my cap.

How sad his death is for our nation!

New York
January 1, 1800

Dear Hannah,
I received your letter of last month, I am sorry for this late reply.
If you think your workday is long, I invite you to become a printer's apprentice. Then you'll know what hard work is. Our shop never closes. We set type during the day and the press runs all night. After a turn at the press, my hands are blistered. Setting type is a great strain on the eyes. We work near the windows for light, but then we freeze. From afternoon on, we work by candlelight.
Our paper just printed an account of the late Mr. Washington's funeral. Have you read about it? He was laid to rest at Mount Vernon. Cannons were fired from a boat in the Potomac River. Companies of soldiers led the procession. The great man's horse, saddled and riderless, walked before the coffin. Mourners and citizens walked behind.
There is more to tell, but I must close. My eyes are tired.
Wishing you improved health, I am,

Your fond brother,
Daniel

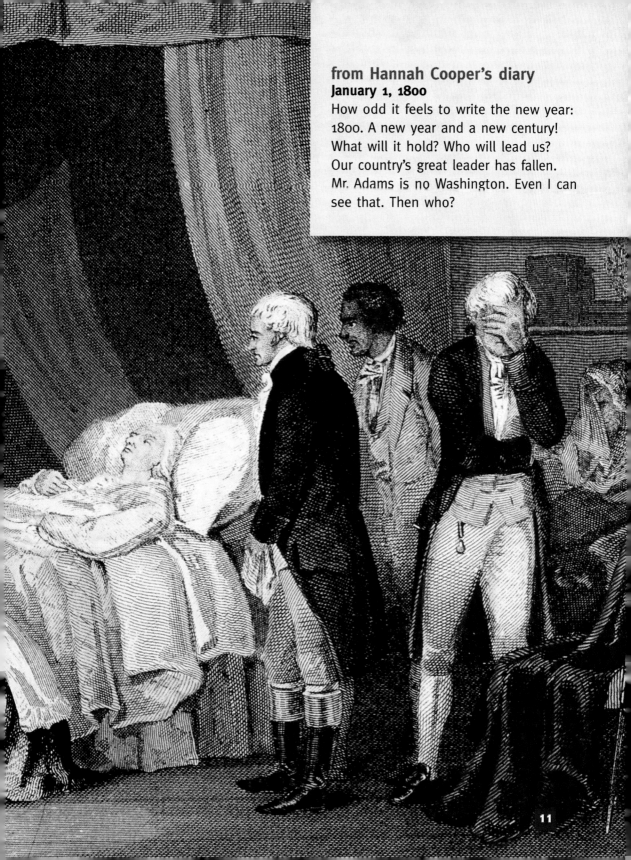

from Hannah Cooper's diary
January 1, 1800
How odd it feels to write the new year:
1800. A new year and a new century!
What will it hold? Who will lead us?
Our country's great leader has fallen.
Mr. Adams is no Washington. Even I can
see that. Then who?

Most Americans felt as Hannah did, that John Adams could not compare with George Washington. Despite his many excellent qualities, Adams was not well-liked or respected.

As the first President, Washington appointed men he trusted to government positions. Then he asked for their advice. This circle of advisers came to be known as the **cabinet**. Not surprisingly, different members of the cabinet—particularly Alexander Hamilton and Thomas Jefferson—often disagreed. These disagreements led to the formation of **political parties.**

Washington was a Federalist. The Federalists believed in a strong central government. The leader of the Federalists was Hamilton. Adams, who had been Washington's Vice President, was also a Federalist. Opposing the Federalists were the Republicans. Jefferson was their leader. The Republicans believed in less power for national government and more freedom for ordinary citizens.

When Washington left office, he warned the nation about the dangers of political parties. That warning didn't stop either party from trying to gain power.

CHAPTER 2

A Shadow Over the Presidency

As the winter of 1800 turned to spring, Hannah settled into the routines of the Presidential household. Overshadowing the details of daily life, however, were two important events coming up in the fall. The first was the Presidential election of 1800. The second was the government's move to the new city of Washington.

The move to Washington meant that very few months remained to pay social visits and give parties. After all, who knew what kind of social life there would be in that swampy **frontier** town? The Executive Mansion became a hub of social activity. Mrs. Adams invited everyone of any importance in the capital to dine.

The upcoming election had a darker effect on the President's household. John Adams was gloomy about his chances of being reelected. Abigail worried about her husband's health and spirits. She was also angry that her husband might be rejected by a nation for which he had worked so hard. Hannah, quiet but observant, took it all in.

Funeral procession of George Washington

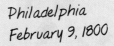

Philadelphia
February 9, 1800

Dear Daniel,
    I am well and hope you are the same. I rise early in the morning now to write before anyone is about, as Mrs. Adams does. She writes a great many letters this way.
    Mr. Adams, I am learning, has a hot temper. Not toward servants and family, but about affairs of government. He reminds me of a pot with a lid on but always in danger of boiling over. I sense that he is not getting along with many in Congress and in his own Cabinet. I also think that he is tired of all the praise for Mr. Washington. I heard Mrs. Adams say that enough has now been done, even for a man such as Washington.
    Our weather has been mild, not at all like a New England winter. When I go to market for Cook, I come home splattered from passing carriages. My shoes and skirt hems are a mess. But I never tire of going, for the people interest me. There are German farmers from the country and Irish storekeepers. The city people talk fast and are always in a great hurry. I think I am beginning to talk faster myself.
    I will close, for I want to write to our parents. Write and tell me how you are.
                  Your ever affectionate sister,
                  Hannah

Philadelphia
February 9, 1800

Dear Mother and Father,

I have only time to write a few lines. Thank you for my Beanie, which arrived safely.

President and Mrs. Adams are in good health. Mrs. Adams asked after you. She sends her regards.

I am very busy. Mrs. Adams has many gentlemen from Congress and their ladies to dine twice each week. She also receives many visitors. It seems we do nothing but cook to feed them all. The President, however, misses his plain New England cooking. So, he asked Mrs. Adams to order bushels of white potatoes and barrels of cider to be sent by ship from New England. They have come. The smell of the potatoes cooking makes me homesick.

I must close. Cook wants me in the kitchen. Wishing you well.

Your loving daughter,
Hannah

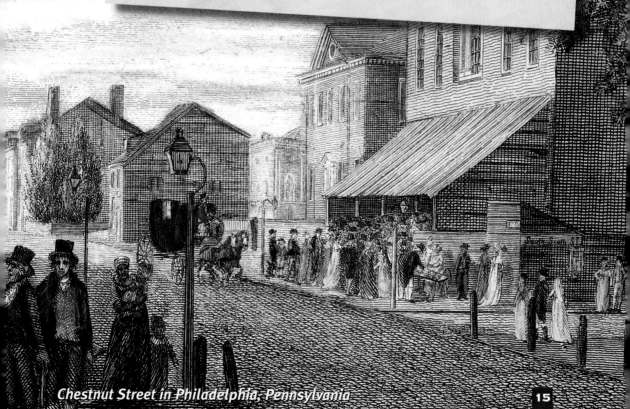

Chestnut Street in Philadelphia, Pennsylvania

from Hannah Cooper's diary
March 3, 1800

Today is my birthday. I am fourteen years old. A package came from my dear parents. It held a set of embroidered handkerchiefs and two bayberry candles. I wept a little from the longing I felt to see them. From Mrs. Adams I received a very pretty shawl.

The weather grows warmer and all around the city the weeping willow is putting out its yellow leaves.

March 12, 1800

Mr. Adams is very angry and moody. I heard him shouting at breakfast. It is being whispered that he has received unsigned letters telling him that men in his own party are plotting against him. They want someone else for President in the fall. I must write to Daniel and ask him why President Adams is so disliked.

New York
March 26, 1800

Dear Hannah,

I am glad you are in good health. I am well, though I often go to bed with tired eyes and an aching head. Master Bartram thinks I may need spectacles. Jenny, his daughter, said spectacles will make me look like a schoolmaster.

I have little sympathy for President Adams and his troubles. Almost two years ago he signed a law called the Sedition Act. This law makes it a crime to write or print anything critical of the government. It is most unfair! Republican newspaper editors everywhere are being hurt by it. Several have been arrested and sent to jail. We all know that Adams is trying to silence all who disagree with his foreign policy.

Here in New York we are worried. Mr. Bartram, who is a Republican, must be very careful. Free speech is our right under the Constitution. This Sedition Act makes it dangerous to exercise that right. We can only hope that the coming election will remove Mr. Adams and the Federalists from power.

Your fond brother,
Daniel

New York
April 16, 1800

Dear Hannah,

Warm weather has returned to this city, too, and with it mud, flies, and bad smells. Ah, Spring!

I have been going to church with the Bartram family. On Sunday I walked home with Jenny. She is a very sensible and intelligent girl. She sometimes helps in the shop when we are busy. Also, she has very nice eyes.

I have learned more about President Adams' policies and why he is plotted against by the other Federalists. It appears his chief enemy is Mr. Alexander Hamilton. Mr. Hamilton dislikes Mr. Adams and thinks he is not fit to be President. He is also against Mr. Adams' foreign policy. Did you know that American ships are fighting a war with France on the high seas? President Adams sent a peace mission to France to try to end this war. Mr. Hamilton is against the mission. Like all Federalists, he mistrusts the French.

You make me happy indeed by your political questions. In return, let me ask: what style of dress are the ladies of the capital wearing this season? I am dying to know!

Fondly,
Daniel

Philadelphia
May 3, 1800

Dear Daniel,

I received your letter of the 16th. Mrs. Adams says the dresses young ladies wear are too thin and short to be decent. Since you were teasing me, I won't tell you more!

I found what you wrote interesting. I am surprised that the Federalists just nominated Mr. Adams to run for reelection. I do hope mean things will not be written about him. He is very sensitive. He is cranky, but I like him.

I will leave for Quincy in about two weeks. Mrs. Adams will come then, too. The President goes to Washington to check on the progress there. I am anxious to see Mother and Father. I only wish you were to be home this summer.

Last night was Mrs. Adams' last party. About 200 gentlemen and ladies were present. Today, 20 to 30 persons are to dine. Last week Mrs. Adams gave a dinner for her youngest son, Thomas. After dining, they moved the tables back and had a dance. It went until midnight! I watched for a time. What fun it would have been to dance, but of course I didn't.

Affectionately, your sister,
Hannah

As Hannah feared, the press was not kind to President Adams. Republican journalists attacked Adams in newspapers, books, and pamphlets. They attacked his policies. They attacked his appearance. They made fun of his size and his fondness for the British king and queen by calling him "His Rotundity."

As soon as Adams was nominated, Hamilton and the Federalists began working to defeat him. They disapproved of his sending a peace mission to France.

The Federalists believed in strong government. They favored Britain over France, where the common people had violently overthrown the king and queen in 1789. The Republicans, on the other hand, were the **champions** of the ordinary citizen. Many looked with approval on the French Revolution and the new government there. Although Adams did not like the French government, he was willing to **negotiate** with it. He knew that his young nation did not have the strength or resources for an all-out war.

Alexander Hamilton

Thomas Jefferson

CHAPTER 3

Summer in Quincy

Abigail Adams left Philadelphia on May 19, 1800. She stopped off in New Jersey and New York to visit her children. In early June she arrived in Quincy with various family members and servants. Hannah was overjoyed to see her parents again after eight months apart.

The summer months in Quincy should have been a time free of worry for everyone, but it wasn't. Hannah worried about her father's health and the family's finances. And the Adamses could not escape the "Election Storm," as Abigail called it. It followed them everywhere, even to their peaceful farm in the country.

Quincy
June 22, 1800

Dear Daniel,

I write to you from our old house. I had forgotten how small and broken down it is. Still, my heart lifted when I saw it. Mother is well. Father suffers with his back. I work for Mrs. Adams at her home, as my wages are badly needed. Do you think you might come here for a visit? It would do Father good.

Mrs. Adams is feeling poorly. She has been working too hard to get the house fixed before the President returns from Washington. He writes that there are no paved streets and few houses. Many of the public buildings are nearly finished.

Mrs. Adams' spirits are depressed, too. Her son, Charles, is very ill in New York. Many false stories are being spread about the President. One story has it that Mr. Adams planned to marry his son to a daughter of King George III. This would reunite the country with Britain. Is it not wrong to spread such lies? Can freedom of the press mean the freedom to publish what is false?

My pen is running away with me. I will close. Write to tell when you will come.

Your sister,
Hannah

The Adams family home in Quincy, Massachusetts

New York
July 7, 1800

Dear Hannah,

I send a few lines to say I will come at the end of this month. After that, the election will give me no time to get away.

You are right about the freedom of the press. It does make men in politics uncomfortable. The Republicans write that Mr. Adams loves the monarchy. They write that Mr. Hamilton is a crook.

What do the Federalist writers say about the Republican candidate, Mr. Jefferson? That he is a revolutionary, a man without morals. That he will turn the United States over to France!

All are false stories, but I don't see Federalists being sent to prison for them. Yet several Republicans who have criticized Mr. Adams are on trial as I write. In closing, I am,

Your Republican brother,
Daniel

from Hannah Cooper's diary
August 4, 1800

Daniel has been and gone. How tall he's grown! I only wish there had been less political talk. Father is a New England man and supports Mr. Adams with all his heart. He has admired him since the Revolution, when Father was but a boy of fourteen. Daniel was full of praise for Mr. Jefferson. He would not stop talking about him, though anyone can see Father is not well. It was most tiresome.

My garden is growing well. It looks like we will have mountains of beans and squash to put up for the winter.

Quincy
August 26, 1800

Dear Daniel,
   We are well as usual. I presume you reached New York safe. It is decided that Mrs. Adams will not join the President in Washington this fall. He is likely to be there but three months (if he loses the election, that is). I will stay on with her here and look after father.
   A stream of politicians have visited Mr. Adams this summer. They are advising him about the election. Father thinks that the Boston Federalists have turned their backs on Mr. Adams. Mrs. Adams' health is better, but her spirits, I think, are low.

Your sister,
Hannah

Abigail Adams was in low spirits that fall for several reasons. She was ill. She was worried about her children. But she was also deeply discouraged by the actions of politicians and the press. It seemed to her that people would say or do anything to win. It was hard to see how this new system of elective government could last.

The election weighed on John Adams as he prepared to go alone to Washington in October. He could hardly bear to be without his wife during such a time. He needed her love and support. At the last minute, he changed his mind and begged her to join him. So, Abigail packed her bags and gathered her people, including Hannah.

President Adams went on ahead in order to reach Washington by November 1. This was the date on which the government was officially supposed to move in. Mrs. Adams and the rest left later and stopped at Philadelphia on the way. They spent two nights at their former home, which had been turned into a hotel. From there, they traveled to Baltimore and then on to the new capital city.

CHAPTER 4

The New American Capital

President Adams arrived in Washington and moved into the President's House right on schedule. All along his journey from Quincy, Adams had been met by crowds of cheering citizens. Their show of support raised his spirits. But the coming election would not be decided by a **popular vote**. Rather, each state had a process for choosing **electors**. Those electors would cast the actual **ballots** for President and Vice President.

At that time, the Constitution said that the **candidate** who got the most votes became President. The one who got the second most votes became Vice President. It was possible that a President and a Vice President could be elected from different parties. This was exactly what happened when Adams was elected in 1796. His Vice President turned out to be Thomas Jefferson, who worked against him tirelessly for four years.

It was 1800. Jefferson was running against Adams again. In those first weeks in the big, empty President's House, John Adams was probably thinking more about his wife than about the election, which he could do little about.

Washington, D.C., 1800

Washington, District of Columbia
November 21, 1800

Dear Daniel,

I write from the President's House in the new capital city.

We had a good journey until we left Baltimore. We took the Frederick Road, which passes through nothing but forest. No village for miles, just here and there a poor cottage. After some miles we took a wrong turn and found ourselves lost. We wandered through the woods for hours on different paths, breaking tree limbs that blocked our way. At last we met a farmer with a horse and cart who kindly guided us back to the road.

Washington is called a city, but in truth it is a wilderness. Our house sits in a sea of mud, tree stumps, and workmen's shacks. Here and there stand houses and public buildings, many unfinished. The Capitol is two miles away.

There are many slaves here. They alone do the physical work. Even the poorest white man won't pick up a shovel or an axe. It is a strange system indeed.

That is all I have time for now.

As always,
Hannah

Washington, District of Columbia
November 23, 1800

Dearest Mother and Father,

I miss you both and think of you often. I do wish you could visit.

The President's house is huge! a castle. Not one room in it is finished. We keep 13 fires going day and night to drive out the damp from the plaster walls, which are still wet. Some of the rooms are large and will one day be glorious. There is an oval room with deep red furniture which is beautiful. The unfinished audience room we use to hang the laundry in. We have but one small back staircase, for the great central stairs have not been built.

Despite the state of the house, we are busy as ever. Gentlemen are forever coming and going or waiting to see the President. Many ladies have called upon Mrs. Adams. This morning a servant came from Mount Vernon with an invitation to visit Mrs. Washington. Would that I could go, too.

Affectionately, your daughter,
Hannah

Abigail Adams and granddaughter watch as a servant hangs wash in the East Room.

New York
December 4, 1800

Dear Hannah,

I am well. You paint a vivid picture indeed of your new home. I read your letter to the Bartrams. They listened with great interest. Jenny said, "Imagine burning thirteen fires at once. Here we have but one to heat the whole house."

Mr. Bartram told us something about the history of the capital city. Mr. George Washington himself chose the spot. The land was surveyed by Mr. Andrew Ellicott, a white man, and Mr. Benjamin Bannaker, a free black man, both from Maryland. The city was designed by a Frenchman, Mr. Pierre L'Enfant. And the President's House was built by workers from many states.

The voting for President begins today. The Republicans have high hopes for victory. Mr. Hamilton recently published a pamphlet in which he attacked Mr. Adams. I confess I don't understand him. He is dividing the Federalists just when they need to pull together if they want to win the election.

Your affectionate brother,
Daniel

from Hannah Cooper's diary
December 8, 1800
Grief and sorrow have settled on this house. The news has come that Mrs. Adams' son, Charles, is dead. He died one week ago in New York. Both the President and Mrs. Adams are stricken with grief, but they must bear up. The election results are coming in from the states. (The first four came today.) When I took Mrs. Adams tea, I offered a few words of sympathy. Poor woman, to lose her son!

from Hannah Cooper's diary

December 16, 1800

The Republicans have won the election!
A postrider brought more results today.
It is certain now that Mr. Adams has lost.
I am sorry for his sake.

Mrs. Adams must be relieved. Soon she
will be able to go home (as I shall!) and
live a quiet, private life. I think the
President is very hurt by his defeat.
He still grieves so for his son. We are
gloomy here indeed.

One year ago I wondered who would
lead our nation into the new century.
Now we know that it will be a new sort
of leader. This leader will defend the
rights of man, not the power of
government—in short, a Republican. Is it
not a wonderful thing that Mr. Adams can
give up his office without bloodshed or
revolution? I know little of government,
but it seems to me that this must be
what our Constitution was meant to do.
I must remember to ask Daniel about it.

December 23, 1800

Results from the last two states—Georgia
and Tennessee—have arrived. Mr.
Jefferson is tied with his running mate,
Mr. Aaron Burr! Both men have 73 votes.
The House of Representatives must vote
to break the tie. I hope Mr. Jefferson is
elected.

*West front of the Capitol,
Washington, D.C.* ▶

Washington, District of Columbia
February 8, 1801

Dear Mother and Father,

I dare say you expect that I am already upon my journey home. I write to say that Mrs. Adams has decided to stay until after the House of Representatives vote for President. She feels she cannot leave without knowing who will be our future leader. The vote begins in three days.

We are packing for the journey. Amidst it all, Mr. Adams keeps busy at his desk. Two weeks ago he appointed Mr. John Marshall as the new Chief Justice of the Supreme Court. You will like that, Father, for he is a strong Federalist. (And, oddly, a cousin to Mr. Jefferson. I hear Mr. J. cannot stand him!) Mr. Adams will stay in Washington until the new President is inaugurated.

Mrs. Adams is dreading the journey, as I am. The roads are so terribly bad at this time of year. There are so many streams and rivers without bridges, that must be crossed. I long for home. With the hope of seeing you before long, I am,

Your loving daughter,
Hannah

The voting in the House of Representatives began on February 11, 1801. As it turned out, Abigail Adams didn't stay in Washington long enough to find out the results. She was in Baltimore by February 13, and in Quincy two weeks later.

Meanwhile, the House of Representatives was unable to break the tie between Jefferson and Burr. The Republicans all backed Jefferson. Burr got votes from the Federalists, who would do anything to keep Jefferson from becoming president. The vote was taken again and again. Day turned to evening and then to night. Between votes, members stretched out on the floor with blankets and pillows sent from home. Others napped at their desks wrapped in coats and shawls.

Six days passed as members tried to persuade Burr supporters to switch their votes. Finally, on the 36th ballot, they succeeded—in a way. Federalist members from three states cast blank ballots. But it was enough to break the tie. Thomas Jefferson was elected the third President of the United States.

CHAPTER 5

A New Beginning

News of the Republican victory of 1800 was greeted all over the 16 states with joy and celebration. Bells were rung and crowds gathered. Republican songs, cheers, and toasts rang out in streets and taverns everywhere. Three cheers for Jefferson and liberty! Good riddance to the Federalists, lovers of Britain and the king, enemies of freedom and France!

The defeated Federalist leaders were glum. Federalist newspapers predicted that the people would run wild, religion would be given up, and the Constitution would be overturned.

However, Abigail Adams was more optimistic. After the first disappointment had worn off, she took a positive view: "Unless the party are more mad and wild than I believe they will be permitted to be," she wrote, "things will not suddenly change."

New York
March 22, 1801

Dear Hannah,

I trust you are well and happy to be home. I was glad to see you when you stopped here on your journey from the capital last month.

The Bartrams liked you very much. Mrs. Bartram was pleased at how handy you were in the kitchen. Jenny loved your stories of Mrs. Adams' parties. She also liked sharing her room with you. It was like having a sister, she said. And you spoke so well of Mr. Adams that I think Mr. Bartram may change his opinion of the man a bit.

Did you read about President Jefferson's inauguration in the papers? He showed himself to be an honest Republican. He walked to his inauguration rather than ride in a fancy carriage. He wore no uniform but an ordinary suit of clothes. His speech expressed fine Republican ideas: that the majority must rule, but the rights of the minority must be protected. Mr. Jefferson will free those writers and editors who were jailed. The army and navy are to be reduced and taxes to be lowered. The American people could not do better, in my opinion.

How is His Rotundity doing in retirement? Let me have a letter soon. I remain,

Your fond brother,

Daniel

Quincy
May 2, 1801

Dear Daniel,

We are well as usual. The weather has turned fine, and the fruit trees are coming into bloom. On warm days, Father sits in the sun. But most days he stays in his bed. I fear he is not long for this world.

Why must you write so meanly about Mr. Adams now? He is no longer President, so stop. He and Mrs. Adams were sad when they came back from Washington. They are recovering their spirits. It helps that they tend to their farm each day. Their house is very full with relatives, visitors, and servants. The table is so crowded that meals remind me of the dinners Mrs. Adams gave as the President's wife. However, the meal itself is only boiled cornmeal and meat.

I think often of changing my situation. I am fifteen now. Shall I be a house servant all my days? But when I ask myself what else I'm fit for, I have no answer. Mother and Father need me close by. I think I must stay where I am forever.

With fond greetings to the Bartrams,

Your sister,

Hannah

Thomas Jefferson hitching his horse before entering the Capitol

from Hannah's diary

July 4, 1801

Father died this morning. May his dear soul find peace at last. Mother is taking it hard, though we knew his end was near. I had little time to grieve before the neighbors arrived to lay out the body. We will have a funeral day after tomorrow. I must write to Daniel. Mrs. Adams visited, bringing food and kind words.

Today is our nation's 25th anniversary of independence. We are truly a nation. If Father were alive, how proud he would be!

August 1, 1801

Daniel is home for three weeks. He told Mother that when he finishes his apprenticeship in one year, he will come home. He will find a situation with a printer, and we'll support Mother together.

Daniel has whispered another idea to me. There is land in the West to be settled, he says, and they need strong men and women. He is dreaming of Ohio. I like the sound of it. Perhaps in a year or two, if I work hard, save my wages...

We shall see.

Two years later, Daniel and Jenny Bartram were married. Then the Coopers—Daniel, Jenny, Hannah, and Mother—set out together for the new state of Ohio. Like many other Americans before and since, they believed they could make a better life in the West.

The Coopers joined a settlement near the Scioto River. Hannah later married, and she and Daniel both had large families. Their mother lived to a ripe old age and was a great-grandmother before she died. Daniel eventually started a newspaper. In 22 years of publication, his **editorials** were always proudly Republican.

John and Abigail Adams lived in Quincy for the rest of their days. Abigail Adams died in 1818. John Adams died on the same day as Thomas Jefferson: July 4, 1826, the fiftieth anniversary of the signing of the Declaration of Independence.

Jefferson's victory over Adams in 1800 was the first transfer of political power from one party to another in our history. It showed Americans that elective government could work—and it continues to work to this day.

Glossary

apprentice - a person who works for a skilled worker in order to learn a trade

ballot - a secret way of voting, such as on a machine or on a slip of paper

cabinet - a group of advisers chosen by the President to be head of different departments of the government

candidate - someone who is running for an office in an election

champion - a supporter of a person or policy

democracy - a way of governing a country in which the people choose their leaders in elections

editorial - an article in a newspaper giving the opinion of the editor or publisher

elector - a member of a special group of voters chosen to elect the U.S. President and Vice President

frontier - the far edge of a country where people are just beginning to settle

negotiate - to bargain or discuss something in order to come to an agreement

pamphlet - a small, thin booklet that usually contains information on one particular topic

political party - an organized group of people with similar political beliefs who try to win elections

popular vote - accepted by the people in general